easy learning

Multiplication and division
bumper book

Ages
7–9

Rachel Axten-Higgs

How to use this book

- Easy Learning bumper books help your child improve basic skills, build confidence and develop a love of learning.
- Find a quiet, comfortable place to work, away from distractions.
- Get into a routine of completing one or two bumper book pages with your child every day.
- Ask your child to circle the star that matches how many questions they have completed every two pages:

Some = half or fewer   Most = more than half   All = all the questions

- The progress certificate at the back of this book will help you and your child keep track of how many have been circled.
- Encourage your child to work through all of the questions eventually, and praise them for completing the progress certificate.

- The ability to recall and use times tables facts is an essential skill and is invaluable for many mathematical processes.
- Learning times tables at an early age gives your child confidence with numbers.

Parent tip
Look out for tips on how to help your child learn.

ACKNOWLEDGEMENTS

Published by Collins
An imprint of HarperCollinsPublishers Ltd
1 London Bridge Street
London SE1 9GF

© HarperCollinsPublishers Limited 2017

ISBN 9780008212421

First published 2017

10 9 8 7 6 5 4 3 2 1

All images and illustrations are
© Shutterstock.com and
© HarperCollinsPublishers

British Library Cataloguing in Publication Data.

A CIP record of this book is available from the British Library.

Author: Rachel Axten-Higgs
Commissioning Editor: Michelle I'Anson
Editor and Project Manager: Rebecca Skinner
Cover Design: Sarah Duxbury
Text Design & Layout: Paul Oates and Q2A Media
Production: Paul Harding
Printed in Great Britain by Martins the Printers

MIX
Paper from responsible sources
FSC™ C007454
www.fsc.org

FSC™ is a non-profit international organisation established to promote the responsible management of the world's forests. Products carrying the FSC label are independently certified to assure consumers that they come from forests that are managed to meet the social, economic and ecological needs of present and future generations, and other controlled sources.

Find out more about HarperCollins and the environment at
www.harpercollins.co.uk/green

HarperCollins
PUBLISHERS
Since 1817
200

Contents

Two, five and ten times tables

1 Write the numbers that will come out of the function machines.

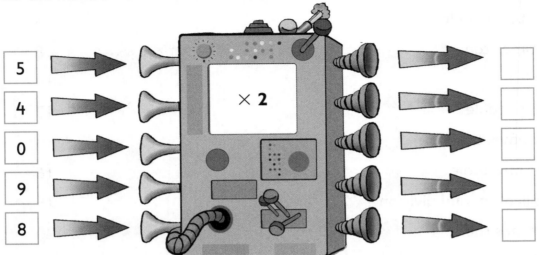

5 → → ☐
4 → × **2** → ☐
0 → → ☐
9 → → ☐
8 → → ☐

2

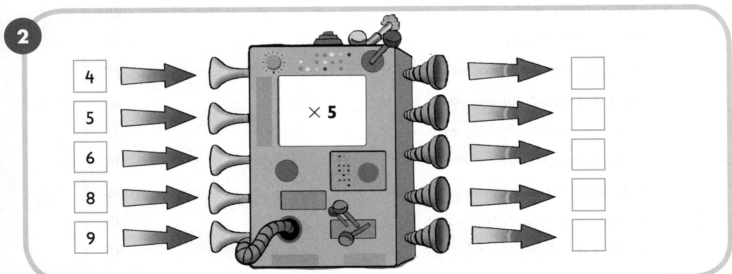

4 → → ☐
5 → × **5** → ☐
6 → → ☐
8 → → ☐
9 → → ☐

3

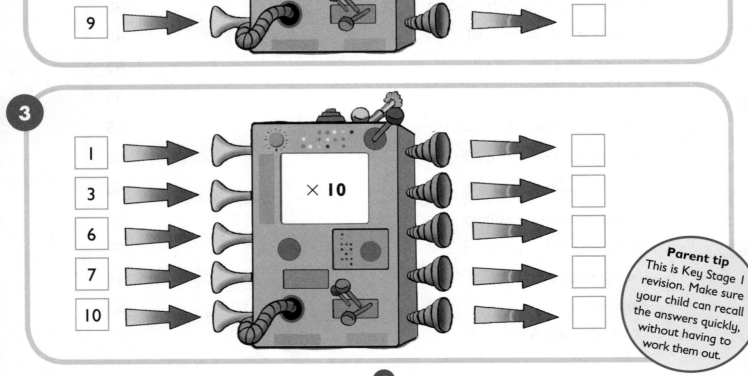

1 → → ☐
3 → × **10** → ☐
6 → → ☐
7 → → ☐
10 → → ☐

Parent tip
This is Key Stage 1 revision. Make sure your child can recall the answers quickly, without having to work them out.

4 Sam eats 5 pieces of fruit every day.
How many pieces of fruit does Sam eat in 9 days?

[ ] pieces of fruit

5 Isobel takes part in a sponsored walk.
She raises £28.
Isobel's gran says she will match that amount to double the total raised.
How much money has Isobel raised now?

£ [ ]

6 On Saturday, Jason cleans cars to raise some money.
He cleans inside and outside and charges £10 for each car.
He cleans 12 cars in total.
How much money does Jason earn?

£ [ ]

How much did you do?   Questions 1–6

Circle the star
to show how much
you have done.

☆ Some   ★ Most   ★ All

Three times table

1 The answers to the three times table are all multiples of 3.
Circle the multiples of 3.

| 3 | 5 | 6 | 7 | 9 | 10 | 12 | 14 | 15 | 16 | 17 |

| 18 | 20 | 21 | 22 | 24 | 25 | 27 | 28 | 30 | 32 | 33 |

2 Draw a line from each multiplication to the answer.

| 3 × 3 |

| 3 × 5 |

| 3 × 7 |

| 3 × 9 |

| 3 × 100 |

| 3 × 10 |

27

30

9

300

15

21

Parent tip
Encourage your child to say the whole multiplication calculation, e.g. 'three times two is six'.

3 Write a number sentence to show the number of wheels in each group of tricycles.

$\boxed{} \times \boxed{3} = \boxed{}$　　$\boxed{} \times \boxed{} = \boxed{}$　　$\boxed{} \times \boxed{} = \boxed{}$

4 Use a blue crayon to colour the pieces that show a multiple of 3.
Leave the other pieces blank.

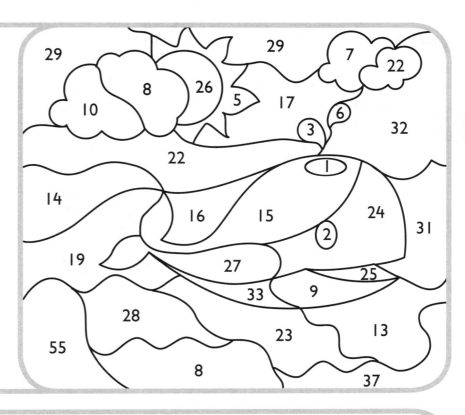

5 A shop charges £3 for a milkshake.
Work out the cost of each quantity.

2 milkshakes	£ ☐	6 milkshakes	£ ☐	
3 milkshakes	£ ☐	8 milkshakes	£ ☐	
5 milkshakes	£ ☐	10 milkshakes	£ ☐	

Parent tip
Use practical situations to help your child learn their times tables.

6 Count on or back in threes. Fill in the missing numbers.

6	☐	12	☐	18	☐
39	☐	33	☐	☐	24
39	☐	45	☐	☐	☐

How much did you do?   Questions 1–6

Circle the star to show how much you have done.

Some   Most   All

Four times table

1 A car has four tyres.
Write a number sentence to show the number of tyres in each group of cars.

□ × 4 = □   □ × □ = □   □ × □ = □

2 The answers in a times table are all multiples of that number.
Circle the multiples of 4.

4	16	8	22	12	26
6	20	24	11	28	15
30	44	36	45	56	41
32	48	50	38	52	40

Parent tip
Make sure your child understands that a multiple of a number is the result of multiplying that number by another whole number.

3 Write the answers.

4 × 2 = □   4 × 5 = □   4 × 0 = □

4 × 7 = □   4 × 8 = □   4 × 9 = □

4 × 10 = □   4 × 4 = □   4 × 3 = □

4 Multiply each number by the centre number.
Write your answers in the outer ring.

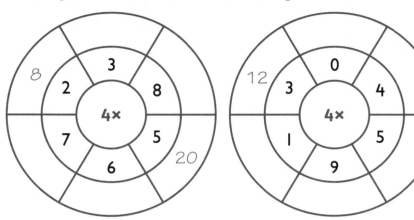
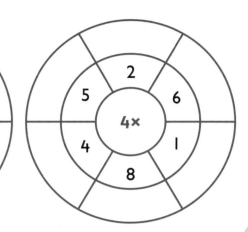

5 Draw a line from each multiplication to the correct answer.

4 × 0	24
4 × 1	12
4 × 3	0
4 × 6	36
4 × 9	4

6 Count on or back in fours. Fill in the missing numbers.

8	☐	16	☐	☐	28
48	☐	40	☐	☐	28
44	☐	☐	☐	60	☐

Multiples

1 Circle multiples of 2 in red, multiples of 3 in green and multiples of 4 in blue.

1	2	3	4	5	6	7	8	9	10
11	12	13	14	15	16	17	18	19	20
21	22	23	24	25	26	27	28	29	30
31	32	33	34	35	36	37	38	39	40

2 Draw a line from each multiplication to the product.

6 × 2	20
9 × 3	28
7 × 4	24
9 × 1	12
5 × 4	9
8 × 3	18
9 × 2	27

3 Fill in the missing numbers.

2	4			10		
3			12	15		
4	8					

4 A shop charges £2 for a small pizza, £3 for a medium pizza and £4 for a large pizza. How much will each order cost?

 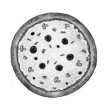 

3 small pizzas £ ☐

5 medium pizzas £ ☐

9 large pizzas £ ☐

4 small pizzas and 2 medium pizzas £ ☐

6 medium pizzas and 3 large pizzas £ ☐

Parent tip
Encourage your child to write a number sentence to help them solve a problem.

5 Colour the picture.
Multiples of 3 = green
Multiples of 4 = blue
Multiples of 5 = black

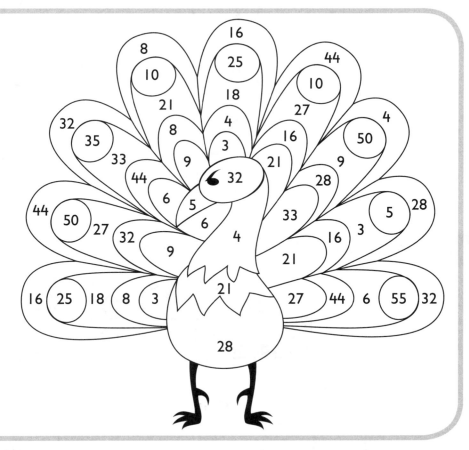

Six times table

The six times table helps you to count in sets of six from zero.

1 Circle the multiples of 6 in the grid below.

(42)	4	13	(18)	(48)	(30)
17	(6)	20	(60)	26	32
(12)	44	(36)	58	(24)	(54)

2 Draw a line from multiplication to the correct product.

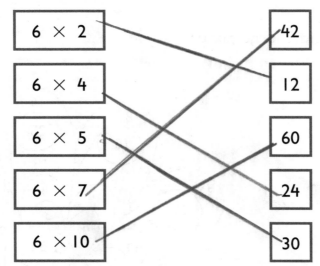

6 × 2	42
6 × 4	12
6 × 5	60
6 × 7	24
6 × 10	30

3 Complete the table to show the numbers that will come out of the function machine.

× 6

In	Out
3	18
6	36
8	48
9	54

In	Out
72	12
5	30
7	42
11	66

4 Count on or back in sixes. Fill in the missing numbers.

0	6	12	18	24	30
48	42	36	30	24	18
42	48	54	60	66	72

5 A scooter costs £6.

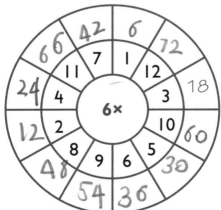

Parent tip
If your child struggles with word problems, encourage them to write a number sentence so they can make the link to their times tables.

Work out the cost of the following quantities.

3 scooters £ 18   5 scooters £ 30

7 scooters £ 4.2   8 scooters £ 48

6 Complete the wheel by multiplying each number by 6.
One has been done for you.

How much did you do?   ## Questions 1–6

Circle the star
to show how much
you have done.

 Some   Most    All

Seven times table

The seven times table helps you to count in sets of seven from zero.

1 Circle the stars that contain multiples of 7.

2 Write the answers.

$7 \times 0 = \boxed{0}$ $7 \times 3 = \boxed{21}$

$7 \times 5 = \boxed{35}$ $7 \times 7 = \boxed{49}$

$7 \times 10 = \boxed{70}$ $7 \times 11 = \boxed{77}$

Parent tip
Remind your child that any number multiplied by zero will be zero.

3 Count on or back in sevens. Fill in the missing numbers.

7	14	21	28	35	42
70	63	56	49	42	35
35	42	49	56	63	70
84	77	70	63	56	49

4 Draw a line to match each multiplication to the correct answer.

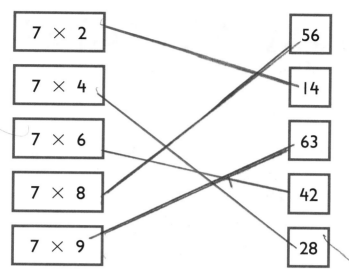

7 × 2		56
7 × 4		14
7 × 6		63
7 × 8		42
7 × 9		28

5 There are 7 days in a week.
Write a number sentence that uses the 7 times table to answer each question.

How many days are there in two weeks? $2 \times 7 = 14$

How many days are there in five weeks? $5 \times 7 = 35$

How many days are there in nine weeks? $9 \times 7 = 63$

6 Multiply each number by 7 to complete the wheel.

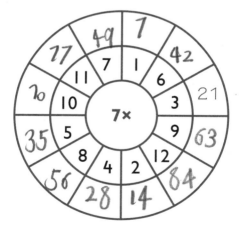

Eight times table

The eight times table helps you to count in sets of eight from zero.

1 Circle all the multiples of 8 in this number square.

1	2	3	4	5	6	7	8	9	10
11	12	13	14	15	16	17	18	19	20
21	22	23	24	25	26	27	28	29	30
31	32	33	34	35	36	37	38	39	40
41	42	43	44	45	46	47	48	49	50
51	52	53	54	55	56	57	58	59	60
61	62	63	64	65	66	67	68	69	70
71	72	73	74	75	76	77	78	79	80

Parent tip
Multiplying by 8 it is the same as doubling the number, doubling the answer, then doubling the answer again (or doubling learned facts from the four times table).

2 Draw a line to match each multiplication to the correct product.

8 × 2		48
8 × 3		80
8 × 8		16
8 × 6		64
8 × 10		24

3 Count on or back in eights. Fill in the missing numbers.

8   24   48

80   64

4 Action figures cost £8 each.
Work out the cost of these quantities.

3 action figures   £ [　]

5 action figures   £ [　]

8 action figures   £ [　]

9 action figures   £ [　]

5 Write the answers to these number sentences.

$4 \times 8 =$ [　] $32 \div 8 =$ [　]

$7 \times 8 =$ [　] $56 \div 8 =$ [　]

$9 \times 8 =$ [　] $72 \div 8 =$ [　]

$0 \times 8 =$ [　] $48 \div 8 =$ [　]

$1 \times 8 =$ [　] $64 \div 8 =$ [　]

6 Freya saves £8 of her pocket money every month.
Work out how long it will take her to save each amount.

£24 [　] months   £56 [　] months

£72 [　] months   £80 [　] months

£96 [　] months   £800 [　] months

How much did you do?   Questions 1-6

Circle the star
to show how much
you have done.

 Some   Most   All

Multiplication and division 1

Multiplication and division are the inverse (opposite) of one another.

1 Draw a line to match each calculation to the correct answer.

6 × 8	18
64 ÷ 8	10
4 × 7	48
49 ÷ 7	45
3 × 6	8
60 ÷ 6	28
5 × 9	7

2 Write one times table fact and one matching division fact for each number.

40   ☐ × ☐ = ☐   64   ☐ × ☐ = ☐
      ☐ ÷ ☐ = ☐   ☐ ÷ ☐ = ☐

63   ☐ × ☐ = ☐   72   ☐ × ☐ = ☐
      ☐ ÷ ☐ = ☐   ☐ ÷ ☐ = ☐

3 Write two division facts using the three numbers from the multiplication fact.

4 × 9 = 36   ☐ ÷ ☐ = ☐   7 × 6 = 42   ☐ ÷ ☐ = ☐
              ☐ ÷ ☐ = ☐   ☐ ÷ ☐ = ☐

3 × 8 = 24   ☐ ÷ ☐ = ☐   4 × 8 = 32   ☐ ÷ ☐ = ☐
              ☐ ÷ ☐ = ☐   ☐ ÷ ☐ = ☐

4 Work out the answer to each calculation.
Use the key to find the colour for that answer.

Key:
3 = yellow   6 = green
4 = blue   7 = red
5 = orange   8 = brown

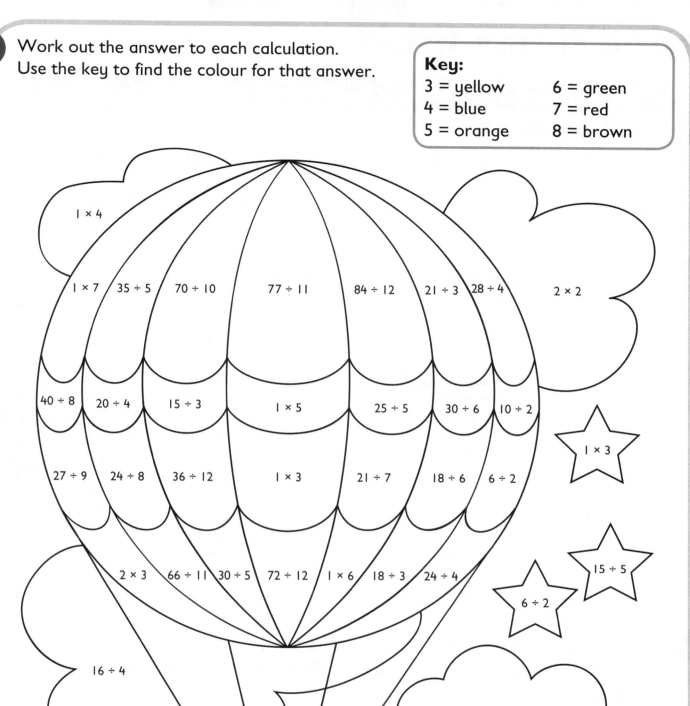

1 × 4

1 × 7   35 ÷ 5   70 ÷ 10   77 ÷ 11   84 ÷ 12   21 ÷ 3   28 ÷ 4   2 × 2

40 ÷ 8   20 ÷ 4   15 ÷ 3   1 × 5   25 ÷ 5   30 ÷ 6   10 ÷ 2

27 ÷ 9   24 ÷ 8   36 ÷ 12   1 × 3   21 ÷ 7   18 ÷ 6   6 ÷ 2

1 × 3

2 × 3   66 ÷ 11   30 ÷ 5   72 ÷ 12   1 × 6   18 ÷ 3   24 ÷ 4

15 ÷ 5

6 ÷ 2

16 ÷ 4

40 ÷ 10

33 ÷ 11

21 ÷ 7

9 ÷ 3

18 ÷ 6

24 ÷ 3

Nine times table

The nine times table helps you to count in sets of nine from zero.

1 Circle the multiples of 9.

9   15   18   21   27   33   36   40   45   51   54   59

63   66   69   72   76   81   85   90   93   99   105   108

2 Draw a line from each multiplication to the correct answer.

9 × 2		63
9 × 4		18
9 × 5		45
9 × 7		81
9 × 9		90
9 × 10		36

Parent tip
Ask children to write the answers to the nine times table in order – what do they notice about the first digits and final digits?

3 A school has a fleet of minibuses. Each minibus holds 9 children.
Write a multiplication to show the number of children that each group of minibuses can carry.

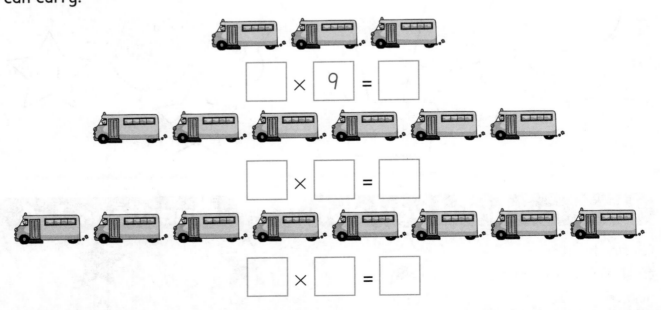

☐ × 9 = ☐

☐ × ☐ = ☐

☐ × ☐ = ☐

20

4 Count on or back in nines. Fill in the missing numbers.

9 ☐   27 ☐ ☐ ☐

99 ☐   81 ☐ ☐ ☐

45 ☐   27 ☐ ☐ ☐

5 School sweatshirts cost £9 each.
Work out the cost of each quantity.

3 sweatshirts £ ☐   7 sweatshirts £ ☐

9 sweatshirts £ ☐   11 sweatshirts £ ☐

6 You can use your fingers to help you remember the nine times table.
Put the finger down that matches the number you are multiplying by 9, e.g.
to multiply 3 by 9, put your third finger down.

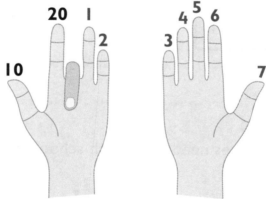

Count the fingers before that one as the tens, e.g. **20**.
Count the fingers after it as units, e.g. **7**.

3 × 9 = **27**

Practise doing this for the nine times table up to 10 × 9.

How much did you do?   # Questions 1–6

Circle the star
to show how much
you have done.   ☆ Some   ★ Most   ★ All

21

Ten times table

1 Circle the multiples of 10.

8   10   15   20   22   30   35   40   48   50   55   60

70   77   80   86   90   100   115   110   118   120   125   130

Parent tip
Point out that multiples of 10 always end with a zero.

2 Draw a line to match each multiplication to the correct answer.

10×5		0
10×3		90
10×8		80
10×0		30
10×9		50

3 Pens are sold in boxes of 10.
Work out the number of boxes needed by each school for each child to have one pen.

A school of 60 children ☐ boxes

A school of 140 children ☐ boxes

A school of 70 children ☐ boxes

A school of 88 children ☐ boxes

A school of 155 children ☐ boxes

4 A shop charges £10 for CDs.

Work out the cost of each quantity.

5 CDs   £ [ ]   9 CDs   £ [ ]

10 CDs   £ [ ]   16 CDs   £ [ ]

25 CDs   £ [ ]   40 CDs   £ [ ]

5 Count on or back in tens. Fill in the missing numbers.

10   [ ]   [ ]   [ ]   50   [ ]

670   [ ]   650   [ ]   [ ]   [ ]

120   [ ]   [ ]   150   [ ]   [ ]

6 Multiply each number by 10 to complete the wheel.

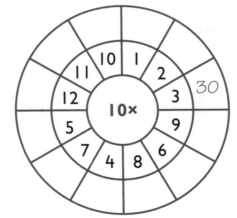

23

Eleven times table

The eleven times table helps you to count in sets of eleven from zero.

1 Circle the multiples of 11.

11   16   22   25   33   38   44   46   55   59   66   70

77   82   88   93   99   105   110   112   121   125   132   143

2 Draw a line from each multiplication to the correct product.

11 × 2	88
11 × 5	55
11 × 6	22
11 × 8	66
11 × 10	110

3 There are 11 players in a football team.
Work out the number of players in each set of teams.

3 football teams [ ] players   6 football teams [ ] players

7 football teams [ ] players   12 football teams [ ] players

9 football teams [ ] players   8 football teams [ ] players

11 football teams [ ] players   10 football teams [ ] players

4 Fill in the missing numbers to complete the wheels.

Wheel 1 (11×): 22, 3, 2, 8, 4, 5, 55, 6

Wheel 2 (11×): 33, 0, 3, 4, 1, 5, 9

Wheel 3 (11×): 2, 5, 6, 7, 11, 8

Wheel 4 (11×): 5, 9, 8, 33, 10, 11

Wheel 5 (11×): 7, 8, 10, 121, 2, 44

Wheel 6 (11×): 55, 9, 132, 3, 7, 4

Wheel 7 (11×): 110, 8, 7, 12, 9, 66

Wheel 8 (11×): 88, 33, 12, 9, 121, 110

Wheel 9 (11×): 132, 3, 11, 88, 7, 11

 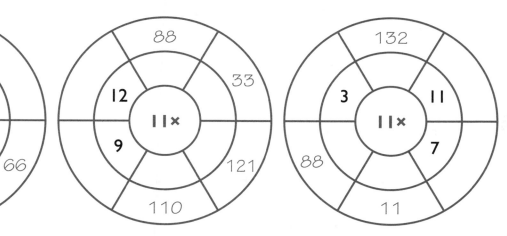

Twelve times table

1 A large egg box contains 12 eggs.
Write a number sentence to show the number of eggs in each group of boxes.

$\boxed{} \times \boxed{12} = \boxed{}$

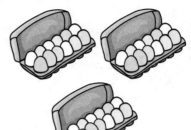

$\boxed{} \times \boxed{} = \boxed{}$

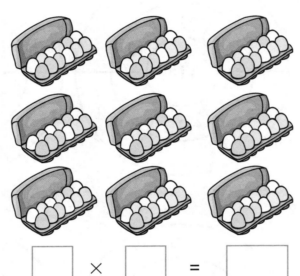

$\boxed{} \times \boxed{} = \boxed{}$

2 Circle the multiples of 12.

12	22	24	30	36	42	48	54	60	64	68	72

84	88	92	96	100	104	108	112	118	120	124	132

3 Write the answers.

$12 \times 2 = \boxed{}$ $12 \times 4 = \boxed{}$ $12 \times 11 = \boxed{}$

$12 \times 8 = \boxed{}$ $12 \times 10 = \boxed{}$ $12 \times 12 = \boxed{}$

4 Fill in the missing numbers to complete the wheels.

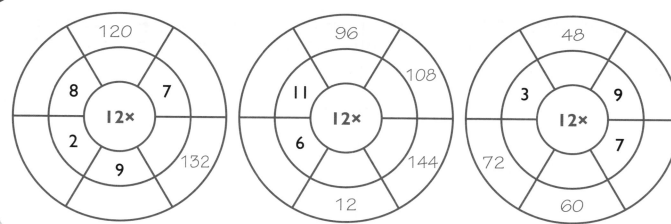

5 Draw a line from each multiplication to the correct answer.

12 × 5	84
12 × 6	72
12 × 7	108
12 × 9	144
12 × 12	60

6 Count on or back in twelves. Fill in the missing numbers.

12   ☐   36   ☐   ☐   72

144   ☐   120   ☐   ☐   ☐

60   ☐   ☐   ☐   12   ☐

Multiplication and division 2

Multiplication and division are the inverse (opposite) of one another.

1 Solve these multiplications and divisions as quickly as you can.

3 × 9 = ☐   9 × 11 = ☐

55 ÷ 11 = ☐   10 × 12 = ☐

7 × 8 = ☐   54 ÷ 9 = ☐

9 × 9 = ☐   7 × 12 = ☐

72 ÷ 6 = ☐   144 ÷ 12 = ☐

2 Fill in the missing numbers in the times tables sequences.

18   ☐   36   ☐   ☐   63

22   ☐   ☐   ☐   66   77

36   ☐   ☐   72   ☐   96

45   54   ☐   ☐   81   ☐

3 Fill in the answer to the multiplication.
Then write two division facts using the three numbers in the completed multiplication.

9 × 8 = ☐   ☐ ÷ ☐ = ☐   ☐ ÷ ☐ = ☐

11 × 7 = ☐   ☐ ÷ ☐ = ☐   ☐ ÷ ☐ = ☐

6 × 12 = ☐   ☐ ÷ ☐ = ☐   ☐ ÷ ☐ = ☐

11 × 12 = ☐   ☐ ÷ ☐ = ☐   ☐ ÷ ☐ = ☐

4 Write one of the inverse calculations to each multiplication.
Example: 3 × 2 = 6, so 6 ÷ 2 = 3

8 × 7 = 56		7 × 2 = 14	
7 × 3 = 21		9 × 3 = 27	
9 × 7 = 63		8 × 6 = 48	
4 × 9 = 36		4 × 4 = 16	
6 × 5 = 30		9 × 5 = 45	
8 × 4 = 32		5 × 5 = 25	
2 × 6 = 12		6 × 9 = 54	
5 × 4 = 20		8 × 9 = 72	
6 × 3 = 18		1 × 8 = 8	
10 × 5 = 50		6 × 4 = 24	
3 × 3 = 9		10 × 8 = 80	

5 Write the inverse calculation to each division.

25 ÷ 5 = 5		16 ÷ 4 = 4	
36 ÷ 6 = 6		9 ÷ 3 = 3	
144 ÷ 12 = 12		121 ÷ 11 = 11	
100 ÷ 10 = 10		81 ÷ 9 = 9	
64 ÷ 8 = 8		49 ÷ 7 = 7	

Mental methods of division

1 When you divide any number by 1, you end up with the number you started with. Write the answers.

$78 \div 1 =$ ☐

$609 \div 1 =$ ☐

$3456 \div 1 =$ ☐

$12905 \div 1 =$ ☐

$103067 \div 1 =$ ☐

2 If you are dividing by 2, you are halving the number.
If it helps, you can partition the number into hundreds, tens and ones and halve each part.

Example: $374 \div 2$

$300 \div 2 = 150 \qquad 70 \div 2 = 35 \qquad 4 \div 2 = 2$

$150 + 35 + 2 = 187$

Write the answers.

$56 \div 2 =$ ☐ $92 \div 2 =$ ☐ $496 \div 2 =$ ☐

$84 \div 2 =$ ☐ $586 \div 2 =$ ☐ $748 \div 2 =$ ☐

3 You can count in steps in your head to help you with division.
It is quicker if you know your times tables!

Example: $56 \div 8$

$56 \div 8 = 7$

$54 \div 6 =$ ☐ $35 \div 7 =$ ☐

$64 \div 8 =$ ☐ $36 \div 9 =$ ☐

Parent tip
It is vital that your child continues to practise their multiplication tables, as it will help them with mental division.

4 Try splitting the number you are dividing.

Example: 48 ÷ 3 = (30 ÷ 3) + (18 ÷ 3) = 10 + 6 = 16

52 ÷ 4 = ☐ + ☐ = ☐ + ☐ = ☐

84 ÷ 6 = ☐ + ☐ = ☐ + ☐ = ☐

91 ÷ 7 = ☐ + ☐ = ☐ + ☐ = ☐

104 ÷ 8 = ☐ + ☐ = ☐ + ☐ = ☐

Parent tip
Your child should split the large number into numbers they are familiar with, e.g. a tens number and a smaller number from their times tables.

5 There are 117 cars in a car park.
The car park has 9 floors, which each hold the same number of cars.
How many cars can park on each floor?

☐ cars

6 In a school there are 144 children.
Each class has the same number of children.
There are 8 classes in total.
How many children are in each class?

☐ children

How much did you do?   Questions 1–6

Circle the star
to show how much
you have done.

 Some

 Most

 All

Multiplying and dividing with 0 and 1

When you multiply by zero, the answer is always zero!

1 Answer these questions as quickly as you can.

$7 \times 0 = \boxed{}$ $10 \times 0 = \boxed{}$ $7 \times 1 = \boxed{}$

$10 \times 1 = \boxed{}$ $9 \times 1 = \boxed{}$ $0 \times 0 = \boxed{}$

$9 \times 0 = \boxed{}$ $1 \times 0 = \boxed{}$ $8 \div 1 = \boxed{}$

$7 \div 1 = \boxed{}$ $45 \div 1 = \boxed{}$ $0 \div 37 = \boxed{}$

2 Work out the answer to each calculation.
If the answer is 0, colour that part of the picture red.
If the answer is not 0, colour that part of the picture yellow.

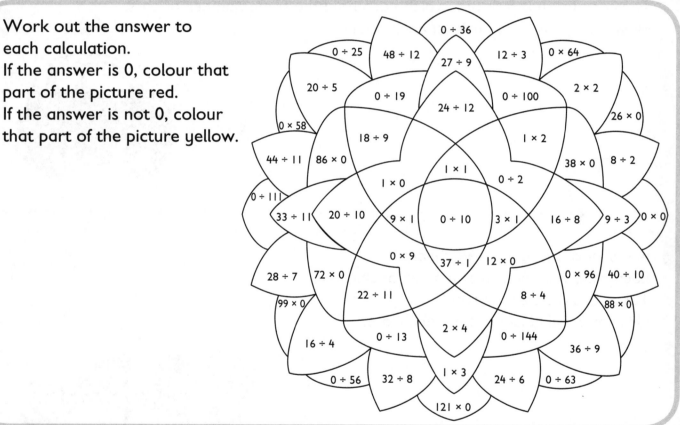

3 Write six multiplication and division number sentences that have an answer of zero.
They must be different from the ones in the picture.

_____   _____

_____   _____

_____   _____

4 Put the numbers into the function machine and write the numbers that come out.

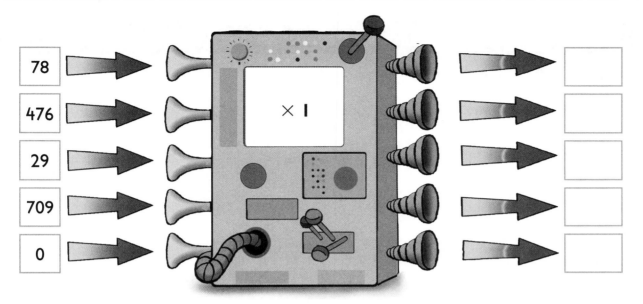

78	
476	
29	
709	
0	

5 Write the answers to these multiplications.

$568 \times 1 =$ ☐ $88 \times 1 =$ ☐

$976 \times 0 =$ ☐ $17 \times 1 =$ ☐

$19 \times 0 =$ ☐ $99 \times 1 =$ ☐

Parent tip
Remind your child that if they multiply or divide by 1, the answer is always the same number that they started with!

6 Write the answers to these divisions.

$18 \div 1 =$ ☐ $45 \div 1 =$ ☐ $703 \div 1 =$ ☐

$0 \div 88 =$ ☐ $678 \div 1 =$ ☐ $0 \div 211 =$ ☐

$587 \div 1 =$ ☐ $0 \div 999 =$ ☐ $1543 \div 1 =$ ☐

How much did you do?   ## Questions 1–6

Circle the star to show how much you have done.

 Some   ☆ Most   All

Multiplying three numbers

Multiply the digits in whichever order you find easiest.

1 Multiply these numbers.

$3 \times 4 \times 1 = \boxed{}$ $3 \times 5 \times 1 = \boxed{}$

$4 \times 6 \times 1 = \boxed{}$ $5 \times 8 \times 1 = \boxed{}$

$7 \times 4 \times 1 = \boxed{}$ $8 \times 7 \times 1 = \boxed{}$

Now try these

$2 \times 3 \times 2 = \boxed{}$ $2 \times 4 \times 2 = \boxed{}$

$2 \times 3 \times 4 = \boxed{}$ $3 \times 3 \times 2 = \boxed{}$

$2 \times 5 \times 6 = \boxed{}$ $2 \times 8 \times 2 = \boxed{}$

$2 \times 9 \times 3 = \boxed{}$ $6 \times 4 \times 2 = \boxed{}$

2 Write the answers.

$(4 \times 2) \times 3 = \boxed{}$ $4 \times (2 \times 3) = \boxed{}$

$(6 \times 9) \times 4 = \boxed{}$ $9 \times (4 \times 6) = \boxed{}$

$(8 \times 6) + 5 = \boxed{}$ $8 + (7 \times 5) = \boxed{}$

$(7 \times 3) - 8 = \boxed{}$ $6 \times (8 - 5) = \boxed{}$

Parent tip
Remind your child that when a calculation has more than one part, they must complete the part in brackets first.

3 Write the answers.

$(5 \times 5) + 2 = \boxed{}$ $5 \times (5 + 2) = \boxed{}$

$(3 \times 3) - 3 = \boxed{}$ $3 \times (3 - 3) = \boxed{}$

4 James and Ahmed play crazy golf 3 times a week during the holiday.
The holiday is 6 weeks long.
Each time they play crazy golf the boys pay £2 altogether.
How much do they spend playing crazy golf?

£ ☐

5 Yona buys 2 packs of stickers each time she goes to the sticker shop.
During the holiday, she goes to the sticker shop 9 times.
Each pack of stickers costs £1.
How much does Yona spend on stickers during
the holiday?

£ ☐

6 A school orders some exercise books.
Each box contains 4 stacks of books.
There are 20 books in each stack.
The school orders 3 boxes of books.
How many books have they ordered altogether?

☐ books

How much did you do? Questions 1–6

Circle the star
to show how much
you have done.

 Some

 Most

 All

Mental methods of multiplication

1 You need to be able to multiply numbers quickly in your head.

You can use your times table facts to help multiply larger numbers.
Use the first multiplication in each pair to help solve the second one.

$3 \times 2 =$ _____ $30 \times 20 =$ _____

$12 \times 5 =$ _____ $12 \times 50 =$ _____

$8 \times 9 =$ _____ $80 \times 9 =$ _____

$7 \times 6 =$ _____ $60 \times 70 =$ _____

Parent tip
Look at the similarities and differences between the answers in each pair of multiplications with your child.

2 Now try these.

$4 \times 2 =$ _____ $40 \times 2 =$ _____ $40 \times 200 =$ _____

$20 \times 4 =$ _____ $40 \times 20 =$ _____ $400 \times 20 =$ _____

$4 \times 200 =$ _____ $200 \times 2 =$ _____ $4000 \times 200 =$ _____

$200 \times 400 =$ _____ $400 \times 40 =$ _____ $2000 \times 400 =$ _____

3 Use your times tables facts to help solve this problem.

At a lacrosse tournament, each team has 12 players.
There are 30 teams competing.
How many players are there at the tournament altogether?

_____ players

4 Partitioning can help when dealing with large numbers.

Example: 156 × 2
100 × 2 = 200   50 × 2 = 100   6 × 2 = 12
200 + 100 + 12 = 312

Parent tip
Partitioning involves breaking a number down into hundreds, tens and ones, e.g. 156 = 100 + 50 + 6.

Write the answers.

234 × 2 = ☐ + ☐ + ☐ = ☐

378 × 2 = ☐ + ☐ + ☐ = ☐

594 × 2 = ☐ + ☐ + ☐ = ☐

673 × 2 = ☐ + ☐ + ☐ = ☐

Parent tip
It might help your child to think of multiplying by 2 as 'doubling'.

5 Partition these numbers before multiplying.

Example: 23 × 4
20 × 4 = 80   3 × 4 = 12
80 + 12 = 92

54 × 3

☐ × ☐ = ☐   ☐ × ☐ = ☐   ☐ + ☐ = ☐

27 × 7

☐ × ☐ = ☐   ☐ × ☐ = ☐   ☐ + ☐ = ☐

6 Try to partition these in your head.

36 × 5 = ☐   47 × 6 = ☐

124 × 2 = ☐   723 × 2 = ☐

How much did you do?   ## Questions 1–6

Circle the star to show how much you have done.

 Some

 Most

 All

Multiplying 2-digits by 1-digit

Don't be put off by large numbers. Look at the individual digits and use your times tables facts.

1 Multiply these numbers in your head as quickly as you can.

$16 \times 7 = \boxed{}$ $18 \times 9 = \boxed{}$

$22 \times 9 = \boxed{}$ $31 \times 7 = \boxed{}$

$7 \times 13 = \boxed{}$ $8 \times 15 = \boxed{}$

Parent tip
If your child is struggling, remind them of the mental methods covered on the previous pages.

2 Complete these short written multiplications.

Example:

```
  3 5
×   5
-----
1 7 5
  2
```

```
  4 7
×   3
-----
```

```
  6 2
×   5
-----
```

```
  8 6
×   4
-----
```

```
  5 4
×   5
-----
```

```
  5 9
×   4
-----
```

Parent tip
In short multiplication, the numbers are arranged in place value columns. Multiply the ones first, then the tens, etc.

3 Now try these.

```
  3 9
×   6
-----
```

```
  2 9
×   7
-----
```

```
  7 4
×   8
-----
```

```
  6 1
×   8
-----
```

```
  5 9
×   9
-----
```

```
  8 3
×   6
-----
```

4 Write each multiplication in columns and then work out the answer.

76 × 6

94 × 4

73 × 8

87 × 3

Parent tip
Make sure your child is confident this method (short multiplication) before they move on to larger numbers.

5 Use short multiplication to solve this problem.

Jenni has a cold.
She buys 7 boxes of tissues.
There are 96 tissues in a box.
How many tissues does Jenni have? ☐ tissues

6 Entry to an amusement park costs £17.
Work out the cost for each group.

A group of 3 people

A group of 4 people

A group of 9 people

How much did you do?   Questions 1-6

Circle the star to show how much you have done.

Some

Most

All

Multiplying 3-digits by 1-digit

You need to practise different written methods of multiplication.

1 Use the grid method to solve these multiplications.

Example: $154 \times 5 = 770$

×	100	50	4
5	500	250	20

$231 \times 3 = \boxed{}$

×	200	30	1
3			

$118 \times 7 = \boxed{}$

×	100	10	8
7			

> **Parent tip**
> In each grid, the large number is partitioned into hundreds, tens and ones on the top row. They are multiplied separately and then the answers are added together.

2 Complete the grids and write the answer.

$232 \times 6 = \boxed{}$

×			

$316 \times 3 = \boxed{}$

×			

$278 \times 3 = \boxed{}$

×			

3 Use the grid method to solve this problem.

There are 148 books on each shelf in a library.
There are 6 shelves in total.
How many books are there altogether? $\boxed{}$ books

×			

4

Use short multiplication to multiply these numbers.

Example:

```
    3 5 6          3 2 8          5 0 4          7 3 2
  ×     3        ×     7        ×     8        ×     4
  1 0 6 8        _____        _____        _____
      1 1

                   7 1 5          2 0 0          8 7 4
                 ×     7        ×     6        ×     5
                 _____        _____        _____
```

5

Now try these.

167 × 8

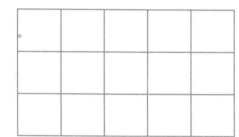

582 × 5

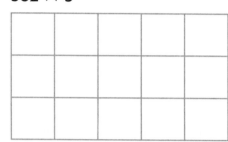

438 × 5

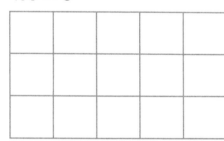

708 × 3

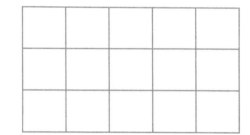

6

Use short multiplication to solve this problem.

A supermarket sells **864** bottles of milk a day.
The supermarket is open **6** days a week.
How much milk do they sell in one week?

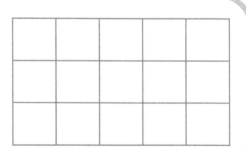

[____] bottles

How much did you do?   Questions 1–6

Circle the star
to show how much
you have done.

 Some   ★ Most   ★ All

41

Factor pairs

1

When multiplied together, the two numbers in a factor pair produce a particular number.

Find all the factors for each number.
List them in order, from smallest to largest.

Example:

24 1, 2, 3, 4, 6, 8, 12, 24 _____

3 _____

15 _____

21 _____

49 _____

---

2 Write one factor pair for each number.

Example: 6 = 3 × 2

15 = ☐ × ☐   21 = ☐ × ☐   49 = ☐ × ☐

---

3 Here is a factor tree.

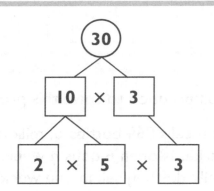

Fill in the missing numbers.

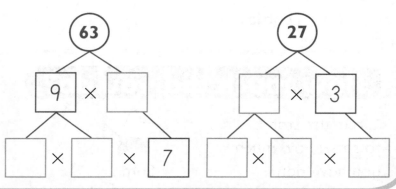

4 List all the factor pairs for the following numbers.

Example:

16   1 × 16   2 × 8   4 × 4 _____

24 _____

33 _____

20 _____

5 You can use factors to help solve multiplications.

Example: 13 × 12
         12 can be broken down to 3 × 2 × 2
         So, 13 × 3 × 2 × 2 = 156

Try breaking the numbers down into factors to solve these multiplications.

17 × 15

_____

14 × 21

_____

6 19 children are doing a sponsored walk.
Along the way they each collect 18 stickers.
How many stickers do the children collect altogether?

[ ]   stickers

How much did you do?   Questions 1–6

Circle the star
to show how much
you have done.

 Some   Most   All

43

Written division

Don't be put off by large numbers. Look at the individual digits and use division facts that you know.

1

Complete these division calculations using mental methods.

$12 \div 6 = \boxed{}$ $32 \div 8 = \boxed{}$

$45 \div 9 = \boxed{}$ $48 \div 6 = \boxed{}$

$21 \div 7 = \boxed{}$ $88 \div 8 = \boxed{}$

2 Complete these short divisions.

Parent tip
The number being divided is written on the right. Divide the tens number first if possible, and then move onto the ones.

Example:

$$7 \overline{)\begin{array}{c} 8 \\ 5\ 6 \end{array}}$$

$$6 \overline{)5\ 4}$$ $$7 \overline{)6\ 3}$$ $$9 \overline{)9\ 9}$$

$$9 \overline{)8\ 1}$$ $$8 \overline{)6\ 4}$$ $$4 \overline{)4\ 8}$$

3 Write each calculation as a short division calculation and then solve it.

$279 \div 9$

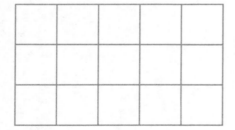

$60 \div 3$

$287 \div 7$

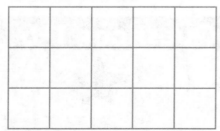

$240 \div 8$

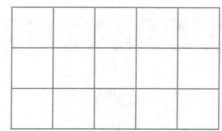

4 Use short division to solve these calculations.
Some of them will have remainders.

Example: $4 \overline{) 3\ 8}$ 9 r2

52 ÷ 4

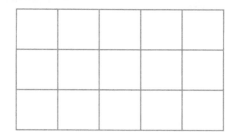

75 ÷ 2

72 ÷ 3

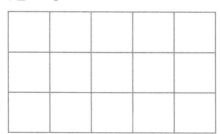

65 ÷ 4

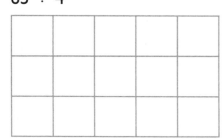

5 Solve these word problems using short division.

Farmer Dray had **78** chickens.
He has **6** coops, which they go into at night.
He puts the same number of chickens in each coop.

How many chickens go into each coop? ⬜ chickens

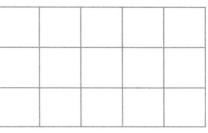

6 Kieran has **98** stickers.

He shares them equally between 5 friends and keeps the remainder for himself.

How many stickers does each friend get? ⬜ stickers

How many stickers does Kieran keep? ⬜ stickers

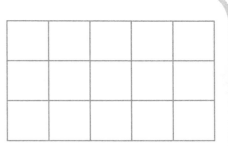

Missing numbers: multiplication

Use your times table facts to find the missing numbers.

1 Fill in the missing numbers.

☐ × 6 = 42   7 × ☐ = 42

9 × ☐ = 45   ☐ × 5 = 45

2 Each toy represents a number.
Work out the number that each toy represents.

 = ☐   × = 9

 = ☐   5 × = 25

 = ☐   × = 40

 = ☐    × = 56

 = ☐   5 × = 30

                         ×  = 42

3 Fill in the missing numbers.

◯ ——→ ×7 ——→ 56

◯ ——→ ×9 ——→ 72

◯ ——→ ×6 ——→ 54

◯ ——→ ×8 ——→ 56

4 Fill in the missing numbers.

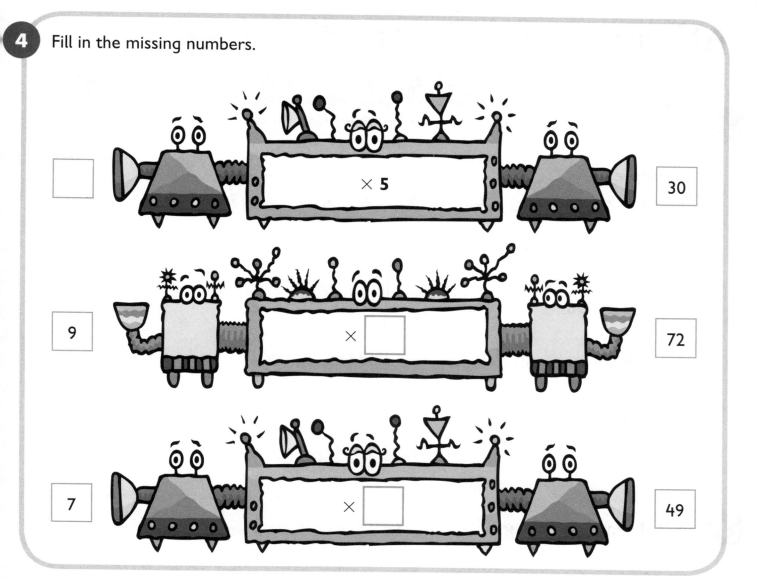

	× 5	30
9	× ☐	72
7	× ☐	49

5

A tray contains 12 doughnuts.
Write the missing numbers.

☐ × 1 = ☐ doughnuts

☐ × 4 = ☐ doughnuts

☐ × ☐ = 84 doughnuts

How much did you do?   Questions 1–5

Circle the star
to show how much
you have done.

 Some

 Most

 All

Missing numbers: division

1 Write two division sentences for each multiplication shown.

Example:

$5 \times 9 = 45$ $45 \div 9 = 5$ $45 \div 5 = 9$

$8 \times 9 = 72$ $\boxed{} \div \boxed{} = \boxed{}$ $\boxed{} \div \boxed{} = \boxed{}$

$7 \times 8 = 56$ $\boxed{} \div \boxed{} = \boxed{}$ $\boxed{} \div \boxed{} = \boxed{}$

$6 \times 9 = \boxed{}$ $\boxed{} \div \boxed{} = \boxed{}$ $\boxed{} \div \boxed{} = \boxed{}$

$7 \times 6 = \boxed{}$ $\boxed{} \div \boxed{} = \boxed{}$ $\boxed{} \div \boxed{} = \boxed{}$

2 Fill in the missing numbers.

$60 \div 6 = \boxed{}$ $20 \div 4 = \boxed{}$

$27 \div \boxed{} = 3$ $25 \div \boxed{} = 5$

$\boxed{} \div 6 = 6$ $\boxed{} \div 9 = 7$

3 Solve these missing number questions as quickly as you can.

$\boxed{} \div 7 = 2$ $77 \div \boxed{} = 7$

$\boxed{} \div 3 = 8$ $\boxed{} \div 4 = 4$

$80 \div \boxed{} = 10$ $110 \div \boxed{} = 11$

4 Work out the missing number in each section.
Use the key to find the colour for that section.

11 × ? = 88

8 × ? = 64

? ÷ 1 = 9

99 ÷ ? = 11

? × 9 = 72

48 ÷ ? = 6

88 ÷ 11 = ?

18 ÷ ? = 2

2 × ? = 16

96 ÷ ? = 12

10 × ? = 80

8 × ? = 72

? × 10 = 90

9 × ? = 36

10 ÷ ? = 2

45 ÷ ? = 5

48 ÷ ? = 12

24 ÷ ? = 3

? × 1 = 8

? × 4 = 32

8 ÷ ? = 1

84 ÷ ? = 12

1 × ? = 8

11 × ? = 33

14 ÷ ? = 2

? ÷ 1 = 8

1 × ? = 3

? ÷ 1 = 4

3 × ? = 9

? × 9 = 27

9 ÷ ? = 3

4 × ? = 12

36 ÷ ? = 12

33 ÷ ? = 11

24 ÷ ? = 3

? × 1 = 4

3 × ? = 18

40 ÷ ? = 10

? × 8 = 32

9 ÷ ? = 3

35 ÷ ? = 5

? × 7 = 35

10 × ? = 30

11 × ? = 44

? × 6 = 42

? × 6 = 24

16 ÷ ? = 4

8 × ? = 56

108 ÷ ? = 12

Key:
3 = red	7 = brown
4 = grey	8 = blue
5 = black	9 = green
6 = yellow	

How much did you do? Questions 1–4

Circle the star
to show how much
you have done.

 Some

Most

All

49

Integer scaling

1 Sam is selling sandwiches for £2 each.
How much do 12 sandwiches cost?

£ [　]

2 Bottles of drink cost 85p each.

Work out the cost of the following quantities.

5 bottles

£ [　]

10 bottles

£ [　]

11 bottles

£ [　]

13 bottles

£ [　]

25 bottles

£ [　]

30 bottles

£ [　]

3 Oscar's toy fire engine is 7 cm long.
He is making a scale drawing that is 13 times bigger.
How long should the fire engine be in his drawing?

[　] cm

4 Freya is making cupcakes.

The recipe makes 12 cupcakes.
It requires the following ingredients:

self-raising flour   150 g
eggs   3
butter   200 g
baking powder   1 tsp
caster sugar   150 g

How much butter does Freya need to make 24 cupcakes?

[   ] g

How much sugar does Freya need to make 36 cupcakes?

[   ] g

How many eggs does Freya need to make 120 cupcakes for a school fair?

[   ] eggs

How much flour does Freya need to make 108 cupcakes?

[   ] g

How much baking powder does Freya need to make 300 cupcakes?

[   ] tsp

How much did you do?   Questions 1–4

Circle the star
to show how much
you have done.

 Some

 Most

 All

Corresponding numbers 1

You need to work out how one item is related to another.

1 A carton of juice sells for 45p.
What is the least number of cartons Greg needs to sell to make £5?

[   ] cartons

2 Raphael is saving up for a computer game that costs £12.
He gets 95p pocket money each week.
If he saves all his money, how many weeks will it be before he can buy the game?

[   ] weeks

3 A pizza restaurant offers 5 different types of topping (ham, cheese, peppers, mushrooms and pepperoni) and 2 different types of base (deep crust and thin crust).
How many different combinations are available if there is only one topping on each pizza?

Parent tip
Encourage your child to draw a table or visual representation of different combinations if they need help.

[   ] combinations

4 Look at the pattern of shapes:

Mila repeats this pattern and continues it.
How many stars will there be when there are 54 shapes in the pattern?

[ ] stars

5 A car park has spaces for 6 motorbikes and these are all full.
How many cars are there if there are 308 tyres in the car park?

[ ] cars

6 A milkshake bar sells 6 flavours of milkshake (banana, strawberry, chocolate, vanilla, toffee and coffee).
Each flavour is available as regular or extra-thick.

How many different combinations are available altogether?

[ ] combinations

How much did you do?   **Questions 1–6**

Circle the star
to show how much
you have done.

 Some   Most   All

Corresponding numbers 2

It is a good idea to make a table to work out different combinations.

1 An ice-cream shop has the following 5 flavours:

strawberry   vanilla   chocolate   mint   toffee

Complete the table to show all the different flavour combinations possible if a customer has 2 scoops of ice-cream.
The two flavours can both be the same, e.g. mint + mint.

Flavour 1	Flavour 2

How many different flavour combinations are possible?

[   ] flavour combinations

The ice-cream shop has the following 3 ways of serving the ice-cream: **tub**, **sugar cone** or **ordinary cone**.

How many different combinations are possible if a customer orders 2 scoops of ice-cream?

[   ] combinations

2 In the Brown family, there is Mum, Dad and three children.
Mum and Dad are the same age.
The combined age of the family is 89.
Find three possible age combinations for the family.

_____

_____

_____

3 A restaurant offers 3 courses for £12.99 when you order from the following menu.

Starter
melon, soup or prawn cocktail

Main
chicken salad, pizza or pasta

Dessert
ice-cream, banoffee pie or cheesecake

If you order a 3-course meal, how many different combinations are possible?

Parent tip
Encourage your child to make a table or list if they need to.

☐ combinations

How much did you do?   **Questions 1–3**

Circle the star
to show how much
you have done.

 Some

 Most

 All

55

Problem-solving

1 Hester has 36 football cards.
She buys 4 more packs, which each contain 6 cards.
How many football cards does she now have in total?

[ ] football cards

2 Mrs Bharaj has 7 children.
Each child has 3 T-shirts.
Mrs Bharaj buys them 6 new T-shirts each for the start of school.
How many T-shirts do the children have altogether now?

[ ] T-shirts

3 On a cake stall, there are 17 plates.
Each plate holds 9 small cakes.
There are also 13 big cakes to sell.
How many cakes does the stall have to sell in total?

[ ] cakes

4 Tennis balls come in tubes of 4.
A tennis academy buys 36 tubes of balls.
They already had 42 balls.
How many balls do they have now?

[ ] tennis balls

5 Aiden's book has 286 pages.
He needs to finish it for book club in 10 days' time.
He has already read 109 pages.
He reads 14 pages a night for the next 9 nights.
How many pages has Aiden read by book club?

[ ] pages

Has Aiden finished the book in time for book club? _____

6 A school has 16 classes.
12 of the classes have 30 pupils each.
In the other four classes, there is a total of 113 children.
How many children are in the school altogether?

[ ] children

How much did you do?   Questions 1–6

Circle the star
to show how much
you have done.

 Some

 Most

 All

Answers

Two, five and ten times tables

Page 4
1 From top to bottom: 10, 8, 0, 18, 16
2 From top to bottom: 20, 25, 30, 40, 45
3 From top to bottom: 10, 30, 60, 70, 100

Page 5
4 45 pieces of fruit
5 £56
6 £120

Three times table

Page 6
1 The following numbers should be circled:
   3, 6, 9, 12, 15, 18, 21, 24, 27, 30, 33
2 $3 \times 3 = 9$, $3 \times 5 = 15$, $3 \times 7 = 21$,
   $3 \times 9 = 27$, $3 \times 100 = 300$, $3 \times 10 = 30$,
3 $2 \times 3 = 6$, $4 \times 3 = 12$ or $3 \times 4 = 12$, $5 \times 3 = 15$
   or $3 \times 5 = 15$

Page 7
4 The parts with the following numbers
   should be coloured blue, showing a picture
   of a whale (all other parts should be left
   blank): 3, 6, 9, 15, 24, 27, 33
5 £6, £18
   £9, £24
   £15, £30
6 9, 15, 21
   36, 30, 37
   42, 48, 51, 54

Four times table

Page 8
1 $1 \times 4 = 4$, $4 \times 4 = 16$, $6 \times 4 = 24$ or $4 \times 6 = 24$
2 The following numbers should be circled:
   4, 8, 12, 16, 20, 24, 28, 32, 36, 40, 44, 48, 52, 56
3 8, 20, 0
   28, 32, 36
   40, 16, 12

Page 9
4
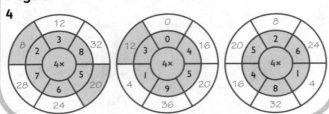

Page 9 (right column)
5 $4 \times 0 = 0$, $4 \times 1 = 4$, $4 \times 3 = 12$,
   $4 \times 6 = 24$, $4 \times 9 = 36$
6 12, 20, 24
   44, 36, 32
   48, 52, 56, 64

Multiples

Page 10
1 The following numbers should be circled in
   red: 2, 4, 6, 8, 10, 12, 14, 16, 18, 20, 22, 24, 26,
   28, 30, 32, 34, 36, 38, 40
   The following numbers should be circled in
   green: 3, 6, 9, 12, 15, 18, 21, 24, 27, 30, 33, 36, 39
   The following numbers should be circled in
   blue: 4, 8, 12, 16, 20, 24, 28, 32, 36, 40
2 $6 \times 2 = 12$, $9 \times 3 = 27$, $7 \times 4 = 28$,
   $9 \times 1 = 9$, $5 \times 4 = 20$, $8 \times 3 = 24$,
   $9 \times 2 = 18$
3 6, 8, 12, 14
   6, 9, 18, 21
   12, 16, 20, 24, 28

Page 11
4 From top to bottom: £6, £15, £36, £14, £30
5 The numbered parts should be coloured as
   follows:
   Green = 3, 6, 9, 18, 21, 27, 33
   Blue = 4, 8, 16, 28, 32, 44
   Black = 5, 10, 25, 35, 50, 55

Six times table

Page 12
1 The following numbers should be circled: 6,
   12, 18, 24, 30, 36, 42, 48, 54, 60
2 $6 \times 2 = 12$, $6 \times 4 = 24$, $6 \times 5 = 30$,
   $6 \times 7 = 42$, $6 \times 10 = 60$
3 First table from top to bottom: 18, 36, 48, 54
   Second table from top to bottom: 2, 5, 7, 11

Page 13
4 6, 12, 24
   42, 36, 30, 18
   48, 54, 60, 72
5 £18, £30
   £42, £48

6

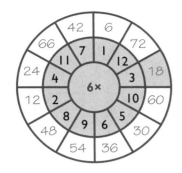

Seven times table

Page 14

1   The following stars should be circled:
    7, 14, 21, 28, 35, 42, 49, 56, 63, 70

2   0, 21
    35, 49
    70, 77

3   14, 21, 35, 42
    63, 56, 42, 35
    42, 49, 63, 70
    77, 70, 56, 49

Page 15

4   $7 \times 2 = 14$, $7 \times 4 = 28$, $7 \times 6 = 42$,
    $7 \times 8 = 56$, $7 \times 9 = 63$

5   From top to bottom: $2 \times 7 = 14$,
    $5 \times 7 = 35$, $7 \times 9 = 63$

6

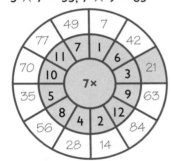

Eight times table

Page 16

1   The following numbers should be circled:
    8, 16, 24, 32, 40, 48, 56, 64, 72, 80

2   $8 \times 2 = 16$, $8 \times 3 = 24$, $8 \times 8 = 64$,
    $8 \times 6 = 48$, $8 \times 10 = 80$

3   16, 32, 40
    72, 56, 48, 40

Page 17

4   From top to bottom: £24, £40, £64, £72

5   32, 4
    56, 7
    72, 9
    0, 6
    8, 8

6   3 months, 7 months
    9 months, 10 months
    12 months, 100 months

Multiplication and division 1

Page 18

1   $6 \times 8 = 48$, $64 \div 8 = 8$, $4 \times 7 = 28$,
    $49 \div 7 = 7$, $3 \times 6 = 18$, $60 \div 6 = 10$,
    $5 \times 9 = 45$

2   8×5 or $5 \times 8 = 40$, $40 \div 5 = 8$ / $40 \div 8 = 5$
    OR 10×4 or $4 \times 10 = 40$, $40 \div 10 = 4$ /
    $40 \div 4 = 10$
    9×7 or $7 \times 9 = 63$, $63 \div 7 = 9$ / $63 \div 9 = 7$
    $8 \times 8 = 64$, $64 \div 8 = 8$
    9×8 or $8 \times 9 = 72$, $72 \div 8 = 9$ / $72 \div 9 = 8$
    OR $6 \times 12 = 72$, $72 \div 12 = 6$ / $72 \div 6 = 12$

3   $36 \div 4 = 9$, $36 \div 9 = 4$
    $42 \div 7 = 6$, $42 \div 6 = 7$
    $24 \div 3 = 8$, $24 \div 8 = 3$
    $32 \div 4 = 8$, $32 \div 8 = 4$

Page 19

4   The parts with the following calculations
    should be coloured blue (4):
    1×4, 2×2, $16 \div 4$, $40 \div 10$
    The parts with the following calculations
    should be coloured yellow (3):
    1×3, $15 \div 5$, $6 \div 2$, $33 \div 11$, $18 \div 6$, $21 \div 7$,
    $9 \div 3$, $27 \div 9$, $24 \div 8$, $36 \div 12$
    The parts with the following calculations
    should be coloured red (7):
    $77 \div 11$, $35 \div 5$, $70 \div 10$, 1×7, $84 \div 12$,
    $21 \div 3$, $28 \div 4$
    The parts with the following calculations
    should be coloured orange (5):
    $40 \div 8$, $20 \div 4$, $15 \div 3$, 1×5, $25 \div 5$, $30 \div 6$,
    $10 \div 2$
    The parts with the following calculations
    should be coloured green (6):
    $72 \div 12$, $66 \div 11$, $30 \div 5$, 2×3, 1×6, $18 \div 3$,
    $24 \div 4$
    The part with the following calculation
    should be coloured brown (8):
    $24 \div 3$

Nine times tables

Page 20

1   The following numbers should be circled:
    9, 18, 27, 36, 45, 54, 63, 72, 81, 90, 99, 108

2   $9 \times 2 = 18$, $9 \times 4 = 36$, $9 \times 5 = 45$,
    $9 \times 7 = 63$, $9 \times 9 = 81$, $9 \times 10 = 90$

3 **From top to bottom:** $3 \times 9 = 27$,
$6 \times 9 = 54$, $8 \times 9 = 72$

Page 21

4 18, 36, 45, 54
90, 72, 63, 54
36, 18, 9, 0

5 £27, £63
£81, £99

Ten times table

Page 22

1 **The following numbers should be circled:**
10, 20, 30, 40, 50, 60, 70, 80, 90, 100, 110, 120, 130

2 $10 \times 5 = 50$, $10 \times 3 = 30$, $10 \times 8 = 80$,
$10 \times 0 = 0$, $10 \times 9 = 90$

3 **From top to bottom:** 6 boxes, 14 boxes
7 boxes, 9 boxes, 16 boxes

Page 23

4 £50, £90
£100, £160
£250, £400

5 20, 30, 40, 60
660, 640, 630, 620
130, 140, 160, 170

6

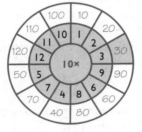

Eleven times table

Page 24

1 **The following numbers should be circled:**
11, 22, 33, 44, 55, 66, 77, 88, 99, 110, 121,
132, 143

2 $11 \times 2 = 22$, $11 \times 5 = 55$, $11 \times 6 = 66$,
$11 \times 8 = 88$, $11 \times 10 = 110$

3 33 players, 66 players
77 players, 132 players
99 players, 88 players
121 players, 110 players

Page 25

4

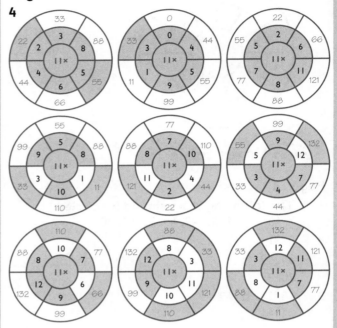

Twelve times table

Page 26

1 $1 \times 12 = 12$, $3 \times 12 = 36$ or $12 \times 3 = 36$,
$9 \times 12 = 108$ or $12 \times 9 = 108$

2 **The following numbers should be circled:**
12, 24, 36, 48, 60, 72, 84, 96, 108, 120, 132

3 24, 48, 132
96, 120, 144

Page 27

4

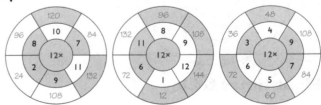

5 $12 \times 5 = 60$, $12 \times 6 = 72$, $12 \times 7 = 84$,
$12 \times 9 = 108$, $12 \times 12 = 144$

6 24, 48, 60
132, 108, 96, 84
48, 36, 24, 0

Multiplication and division 2

Page 28

1 27, 99
5, 120
56, 6
81, 84
12, 12

2 27, 45, 54
33, 44, 55
48, 60, 84
63, 72, 90

3 $9 \times 8 = 72, 72 \div 9 = 8, 72 \div 8 = 9$,
$11 \times 7 = 77, 77 \div 11 = 7, 77 \div 7 = 11$
$6 \times 12 = 72, 72 \div 6 = 12, 72 \div 12 = 6$
$11 \times 12 = 132, 132 \div 11 = 12, 132 \div 12 = 11$

Page 29

4 $56 \div 8 = 7 / 56 \div 7 = 8, 14 \div 7 = 2 /$
$14 \div 2 = 7$
$21 \div 3 = 7 / 21 \div 7 = 3, 27 \div 9 = 3 /$
$27 \div 3 = 9$
$63 \div 7 = 9 / 63 \div 9 = 7, 48 \div 8 = 6 /$
$48 \div 6 = 8$
$36 \div 9 = 4 / 36 \div 4 = 9, 16 \div 4 = 4$
$30 \div 6 = 5 / 30 \div 5 = 6, 45 \div 9 = 5 /$
$45 \div 5 = 9$
$32 \div 8 = 4 / 32 \div 4 = 8, 25 \div 5 = 5$
$12 \div 2 = 6 / 12 \div 6 = 2, 54 \div 6 = 9 /$
$54 \div 9 = 6$
$20 \div 5 = 4 / 20 \div 4 = 5, 72 \div 8 = 9 /$
$72 \div 9 = 8$
$18 \div 6 = 3 / 18 \div 3 = 6, 8 \div 8 = 1$
$50 \div 10 = 5 / 50 \div 5 = 10, 24 \div 6 = 4 /$
$24 \div 4 = 6$
$9 \div 3 = 3, 80 \div 10 = 8 / 80 \div 8 = 10$

5 $5 \times 5 = 25, 4 \times 4 = 16$
$6 \times 6 = 36, 3 \times 3 = 9$
$12 \times 12 = 144, 11 \times 11 = 121$
$10 \times 10 = 100, 9 \times 9 = 81$
$8 \times 8 = 64, 7 \times 7 = 49$

Mental methods of division

Page 30

1 **From top to bottom:** 78, 609, 3456, 12 905, 103 067

2 28, 46, 248
42, 293, 374

3 9, 5, 8, 4

Page 31

4 **Accept other successful ways of splitting the number being divided:**
$52 \div 4 = (40 \div 4) + (12 \div 4) = 10 + 3 = 13$
$84 \div 6 = (60 \div 6) + (24 \div 6) = 10 + 4 = 14$
$91 \div 7 = (70 \div 7) + (21 \div 7) = 10 + 3 = 13$
$104 \div 8 = (80 \div 8) + (24 \div 8) = 10 + 3 = 13$

5 13 cars

6 18 children

Multiplying and dividing with 0 and 1

Page 32

1 0, 0, 7
10, 9, 0
0, 0, 8
7, 45, 0

2 Any part with a calculation involving zero (0) should be coloured red. All other parts should be coloured yellow.

3 Six multiplications and divisions written with zeros in them to give an answer of zero. The zero can be either number in a multiplication; it can only be the number being divided in a division (you can't divide by 0).

Page 33

4 **From top to bottom:** 78, 476, 29, 709, 0

5 568, 88, 0, 17, 0, 99

6 18, 45, 703
0, 678, 0
587, 0, 1543

Multiplying three numbers

Page 34

1 12, 15
24, 40
28, 56
12, 16
24, 18
60, 32
54, 48

2 24, 24
216, 216
53, 43
13, 18

3 27, 35
6, 0

Page 35

4 $3 \times 6 \times 2 = £36$

5 $2 \times 9 \times 1 = £18$

6 $4 \times 20 \times 3 = 240$ books

Mental methods of multiplication

Page 36

1 6, 600
60, 600
72, 720
42, 4200

2   8, 80, 8000
    80, 800, 8000
    800, 400, 800 000
    80 000, 16 000, 800 000

3   360 players

Page 37

4   400 + 60 + 8 = 468
    600 + 140 + 16 = 756
    1000 + 180 + 8 = 1188
    1200 + 140 + 6 = 1346

5   50 × 3 = 150, 4 × 3 = 12, 150 + 12 = 162
    20 × 7 = 140, 7 × 7 = 49, 140 + 49 = 189

6   180, 282, 248, 1446

Multiplying 2-digits by 1-digit

Page 38

1   112, 162
    198, 217
    91, 120

2   141, 310
    344, 270, 236

3   234, 203, 592
    488, 531, 498

Page 39

4   456, 376
    584, 261

5   672 tissues

6   £51, £68, £153

Multiplying 3-digits by 1-digit

Page 40

1   **From top to bottom:** 600 + 90 + 3 = 693,
    700 + 70 + 56 = 826

2   **From top to bottom:** 1200 + 180 + 12 = 1392,
    900 + 30 + 18 = 948, 600 + 210 + 24 = 834

3   888 books

Page 41

4   2296, 4032, 2928
    5005, 1200, 4370

5   1336, 2910
    2190, 2124

6   5184 bottles

Factor pairs

Page 42

1   1, 3
    1, 3, 5, 15
    1, 3, 7, 21
    1, 7, 49

2   **The following pairs of numbers can be written either way round:** 5 × 3 or 1 × 15, 7 × 3 or 1 × 21, 7 × 7 or 1 × 49

3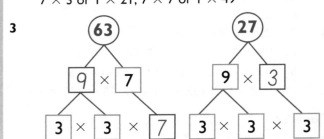

Page 43

4   1 × 24, 2 × 12, 3 × 8, 4 × 6
    1 × 33, 3 × 11
    1 × 20, 2 × 10, 4 × 5

5   **From top to bottom:** 17 × 3 × 5 = 255,
    2 × 7 × 3 × 7 = 294

6   342 stickers

Written division

Page 44

1   2, 4
    5, 8
    3, 11

2   9, 9, 11
    9, 8, 12

3   31, 20
    41, 30

Page 45

4   13, 37 r1
    24, 16 r1

5   13 chickens

6   19 stickers, 3 stickers

Missing numbers: multiplication

Page 46

1   7, 6
    5, 9

2   **From top to bottom:** beach ball = 3, space hopper = 5, car = 8, wind-up toy = 7, guitar = 6

3   **From top to bottom:** 8, 8, 9, 7

Page 47

4   **From top to bottom:** 6, 8, 7

5   **From top to bottom:** 12, 48, 7

Missing numbers: division

Page 48

1   **The divisions can be given in any order:**
    $72 \div 9 = 8, 72 \div 8 = 9$
    $56 \div 7 = 8, 56 \div 8 = 7$
    $6 \times 9 = 54, 54 \div 9 = 6, 54 \div 6 = 9$
    $7 \times 6 = 42, 42 \div 6 = 7, 42 \div 7 = 6$

2   10, 5
    9, 5
    36, 63

3   14, 11
    24, 16
    8, 10

Page 49

4

Integer scaling

Page 50

1   £24
2   £4.25, £8.50, £9.35
    £11.05, £21.25, £25.50
3   91 cm

Page 51

4   **From top to bottom:** 400 g butter, 450 g sugar,
    30 eggs, 1350 g flour, 25 tsp baking powder

Corresponding numbers 1

Page 52

1   12 cartons
2   13 weeks
3   $(5 \times 2 =)$ 10 combinations

Page 53

4   $(54 \div 9 = 6, 6 \times 3 =)$ 18 stars
5   $((308 - 12) \div 4 =)$ 74 cars
6   $(6 \times 2 =)$ 12 combinations

Corresponding numbers 2

Page 54

1

Flavour 1	Flavour 2
strawberry	strawberry
strawberry	vanilla
strawberry	chocolate
strawberry	mint
strawberry	toffee
vanilla	vanilla
vanilla	chocolate
vanilla	mint
vanilla	toffee
chocolate	chocolate
chocolate	mint
chocolate	toffee
mint	mint
mint	toffee
toffee	toffee

$(5 + 4 + 3 + 2 + 1 =)$ 15 flavour combinations
$(15 \times 3 =)$ 45 combinations

Page 55

2   Any combination where the two adults are the
    same age and the five ages add up to 89, e.g.
    $34 + 34 + 10 + 6 + 5$
    $30 + 30 + 10 + 10 + 9$
    $40 + 40 + 5 + 3 + 1$

3   $(3 \times 3 \times 3 =)$ 27 combinations

Problem-solving

Page 56

1   $36 + (4 \times 6) = 60$ football cards
2   $7 \times 9 = 63$ T-shirts
3   $(17 \times 9) + 13 = 166$ cakes

Page 57

4   $(36 \times 4) + 42 = 186$ tennis balls
5   $(14 \times 9) + 109 = 235$ pages, No
6   $(12 \times 30) + 113 = 473$ children

Check your progress

- Shade in the stars on the progress certificate to show how much you did. Shade one star for every ⭐ you circled in this book.

- If you have shaded fewer than 20 stars go back to the pages where you circled Some ☆ or Most ⭐ and try those pages again.

- If you have shaded 20 or more stars, well done!

✂ -

Collins Easy Learning Multiplication and division bumper book Ages 7–9

Progress certificate
to

Name _____   Date _____

pages 4–5	pages 6–7	pages 8–9	pages 10–11	pages 12–13	pages 14–15	pages 16–17	pages 18–19	pages 20–21
☆ 1	☆ 2	☆ 3	☆ 4	☆ 5	☆ 6	☆ 7	☆ 8	☆ 9

pages 22–23	pages 24–25	pages 26–27	pages 28–29	pages 30–31	pages 32–33	pages 34–35	pages 36–37	pages 38–39
☆ 10	☆ 11	☆ 12	☆ 13	☆ 14	☆ 15	☆ 16	☆ 17	☆ 18

pages 40–41	pages 42–43	pages 44–45	pages 46–47	pages 48–49	pages 50–51	pages 52–53	pages 54–55	pages 56–57
☆ 19	☆ 20	☆ 21	☆ 22	☆ 23	☆ 24	☆ 25	☆ 26	☆ 27